A Poetry collection by Starchild
Morgan Guyton

Shipwrecked
Viking

Wider Perspectives Publishing ¤ 2025 ¤ Hampton Roads, Va.

The poems, and writings in this book are the creations and property of Morgan Guyton, the author is responsible for them as such. Wider Perspectives Publishing reserves 1st run rights to this material in this form, all rights revert to author upon delivery. Author reserves all rights thereafter: Do not reproduce without permission except Fair Use practices for approved promotion or educational purposes. Author may redistribute, whole or in part, at will, for example submission to anthologies or contests.

Editing services provided by Crickyt J. Meyer

© 2025, Morgan Guyton, including writing as Starchild
1ˢᵗ run complete in July 2025 Wider Perspectives Publishing, Hampton Roads, Va.
ISBN 978-1-964531-01-4

CONTENTS

SHIPWRECKED VIKING	1
MIXED RACE BATHING IN EAST TENNESSEE	4
I SHIT BLOOD	7
UNPUBLISHED MANUSCRIPTS	10
PAPER SAILBOAT	11
THE DEVIL WAS EXHAUSTED	13
WE WILL NOT LORD IT OVER THEM	15
HEAVEN'S INVASION	16
CUDDLE KINGDOM	18
JALAPEÑO HUMMUS	20
YOU ARE NOT AWAKE	21
THE SERPENT SPEAKS	23
WE DON'T DISLIKE YOU PER SE	26
BEAR	27
WHAT THEY HATE	28
MANDATORY BULLYING	29
FINDING OUR VOICE	30
PINK UNICORN BACKPACK	31
PLYWOOD	33
SEPARATION WALL	35
ROLLO THE VIKING	36
DRUID	40
MAKING EMPIRE GREAT AGAIN	43
A GOD WHO LETS ME EAT HIM	46
PRINCE OF THIS WORLD	51
DANGEROUS	56
THE WITCH	59
THE VALLEY	62
SHE IS RISING	64
I WISH	66
BROTHER'S KEEPER	67

STONE	68
WHEN THEY LOSE THEIR WORDS	70
MESSY MESSIAH	71
OUR GOALIE JESUS	73
PILGRIMS PASSING THROUGH	75
MAY THIS BE THE YEAR	78
THE SPELL	80
FINAL JUDGMENT	81
WINESKINS	82
EYE OF GOD	85
DIVINITY	86
LAVENDER BERGAMOT	87
DEAD END FOR ABRAHAM	89
PYRAMID OF SHIT	91
MY DREAMS	92
MANY GODS	93
THE FATHER	94
EACH OF YOU	96
THE HOST OF THE PARTY	98
REVEREND DOCTOR BISHOP	100
PELAGIUS	101
MOST IMPORTANT TEACHER	103
MAKING PEACE WITH LUCIFER	104
OH FACEBOOK	106
OH PAUL	109
MIRIAM THE TOWER CARD	112
PRECOCIOUS GIRL	115
A GROUP CALLED LOVER	117
PACHAMAMA	118
PLOWSHARES	121
PLEDGE OF ALLEGIANCE	122
GOLIATH	123
SHOES ON THE BEACH	124
YOUR WRATH	125
ANOINTING OF THE WILD GOD	127

STRANGE NERDS	128
SALVATION ISSUE	131
TONGUES OF FIRE	133
POPULAR	136
THIS TOO IS THE REAL WORLD	138
THE WORLD DOES NOT NEED YOUR APOLOGY	140
YOU DESERVE TO BE WORSHIPED	143
CHOPPING CELERY	145
EXUBERANCE AND ACCEPTANCE	148
SONGS OF THE DEAD	149
PANTHEON	150
WHEN THERE IS ONLY ONE	151
ZION	152
NEW SCRIPTURES	154
NEW PENTECOST	157
NEW WORLD	159
IT'S DIFFERENT THIS TIME	161
TO OBEY LOVE	164
LECTIO DIVINA	166
AFTER THE TRIBULATION	167
MY BODY IS A TEMPLE	169
MY BUTTERFLY QUEEN	171
BELOVED CHILD	172

SHIPWRECKED VIKING

Some days
the couch wins
and I keep sabbath
like the tools
oxidizing in my yard.

I am not different
than any other refuse
of empire crumbling
in parking lots
at every intersection.

I am a shipwrecked Viking
slouching overweight
amidst the loot my ancestors
stole without the wars
that gave them glory.

Something in me needs
to smash or build,
but I can't
figure out which
remote to use.

One day will I finally
rush into the snow
on all fours and rage
through the woods till
every tooth is broken?

What am I becoming?
A pusher of buttons,
a connoisseur of prestamped
envelopes and personal
sounding subject lines?

The couch is trying
to eat me: one day
my crumbs will be found
stuffed beneath
the armrests.

How many white men
die this way, having
lost the will to fight
for dreams that require
sailing the open sea?

The frames flash in front
of us and we live
our lives in other peoples'
stories because our own
didn't make the cut.

We are curating
the brand that selected
us to sit in its bleachers
and spell its name on TV.

One day I will embrace
being nobody instead of
tantruming like a condemned
man whose cage is opened
for his final walk.

But more decisive failures
will be required
before I relax while
clicking through my shows,
dissolving into the couch.

A Viking warrior paces
back and forth through my mind;
he will find a way to
pick the lock and
burst into the world again.

MIXED RACE BATHING IN EAST TENNESSEE

I've been to pools
with black people
before

There were
five maybe six
not twenty

And all of them teenagers
pushing and running
where are the parents

Several white men
sit in chairs avoiding
eye contact

I'm not racist
I didn't say you were
I've got small children

So do I
There is nothing wrong here
There is absolutely nothing wrong here

Because teenagers push
and do cannon balls
and yell and taunt and scream

I was a white teenager once
I was loud
sometimes

My youngest son is not
a strong swimmer
these waves

Someone will
be that white parent
go to the desk

Maybe the cops will come
because teenagers are
acting like teenagers

Should I go back and
get my cellphone
just in case

I was a teacher once
It was my job to tell
black kids I didn't know

To settle down
I had a teacher voice
once

And then a white girl
gets a beach ball
my son is laughing

The white people
toss the beach ball
in the shallow end

We hear the shrieks
and splashes
I cannot read

The faces
of the other white parents
they seem relaxed

I am not racist
I just don't want my
son to drown

I was a teenager once
I last did a
cannonball

Back in the nineties
now I don't know
what to do

In crowded pools
so I watch
other people's children

And try to smile
I'm glad that they're safe
I'm glad they can be

Teenagers acting
like teenagers
grabbing pushing running shrieking

My son is laughing
soon he'll be a teenager, too
though he is white

I SHIT BLOOD

I shit blood
because I still eat
spanakopita sometimes.

I shit blood
because this is what happens
when you put a star
inside a human body.

I shit blood
because this is how
a goddess menstruates
when she's trapped inside a man.

I shit blood
because my father made damn sure
his boy didn't grow up to be gay.

I shit blood
because I can't stop
watching children in Gaza
starve to death.

I shit blood
because I wanted Jesus
to come back in the eclipse
and bitchslap every Christian
who's been lusting for the end times.

I shit blood
because I fantasize
about absorbing the sun
into my eyes and lighting up
a phalanx of riot cops
on Armageddon Day.

I shit blood
because I was supposed to be
Freddy Mercury by now
but I abandoned my dreams
to be a good father and husband.

I shit blood
because I'm the bastard child
of Charlemange and my boots
are caked in burial mounds
I stumbled over.

I shit blood
because all my friends
blocked me from spamming
them with late night poetry.

I shit blood
because I'm trying so hard
not to want to be
the hero of the story
I was pushed out of
the way of being.

I shit blood
because you rolled your eyes
and scored me a 7 out of 10
without hearing a single word.

I shit blood
because you and I
have a dynamic and
I could not fawn you Into friendship.

I shit blood
because I only raise my voice
at inanimate objects.

I shit blood
because I've been studying
your face my entire life
and I still don't get your cues.

I shit blood
because Jesus is crucified
in my colon every day.

I shit blood
because Lucifer never stops
trying to take over my heart.

UNPUBLISHED MANUSCRIPTS

When my father dies,
several unpublished
book length manuscripts
of dreams will remain
on the hard drives
of laptops that stopped
charging decades ago,
and I will continue
forgiving myself for not
building a movement
out of his dreams
and maybe I will
learn not to grieve
unpublished manuscripts.

PAPER SAILBOAT

We're dropping you off
at college in two weeks
and it feels like throwing
a paper sailboat into the ocean
or kicking a baby bird
out of the nest
and holding my breath
until your wings flap
for the first time.

I'm trying not to remember
the time I was trying
to teach you how to hammer
a nail and when you felt
my hand on top of yours,
your hand went limp to
let me do all the work.

Or your fourth grade year
when you hid under your hoodie
in the back of the class in
that New Orleans charter school
where we never should have sent you.

Or the time I took you
to the high school football game
and I saw you walk over
to some kids who seemed nerdy
enough for you to say a few
words to them but they didn't
open their molecule to let you
inside so you just looked at
the ground and kept walking.

I'm trying to remember the way
your eyes gleam when you
tell me your latest story idea,
the way you cackle when
you're pacing around the
living room watching YouTube,
the way you quietly fill the
water bottles and mow the
grass and put away the groceries,
the way you take out your phone
and snap photos of clouds and
stairwells and plants that look
like weeds to everyone except you.

You say you're terrified and
excited at the same time.
I told you in the pool several
nights ago that you're
the hero of my movie.

I just want the world
to say yes to you
and I wish a dove would
come down from heaven
so everyone could see
that you are my beloved child
and I delight in you.

THE DEVIL WAS EXHAUSTED

The devil was exhausted,
having spent centuries
consolidating his power:

co-opting every story about
God into colonial conquest
justified by inerrant scripture,

incarnating himself into
self-righteous, hypervigilant
mobs by stirring up hysteria
about the weird kids,

pounding out diatribes
on millions of keyboards
at once to build a lake
of fire with mutual scorn and
sanctimonious pearl-clutching,

handing all the kingdoms
of the earth to geriatric
narcissists and their legions
of flag waving patriots.

He sat on the heavenly throne
before the rapturous worship
of the multitudes who had
crowned him their God,

having crucified Jesus in
every imaginable way in
every queer and brown body,

but even in his absolute victory,
he could not feel the satisfaction
he thought he would taste,

so he cried out again to
the God whose abandoned
throne he had usurped:
*"Why aren't you doing
anything to try and stop me?"*

WE WILL NOT LORD IT OVER THEM

We will not lord it over them
when we supervise
their return to the closet.
As long as they are compliant
in dumping out their pills,
their deviant toys,
and their inappropriate fashion,
the guns will stay holstered.

We understand it's not
their fault that they didn't
have strong fathers to show
them, which is why they will
be given new mentors to
teach them how to fish,
how to build things, and if
they prove trustworthy,
how to use a gun.

Some will be stubborn so
we will have to pull them
aside not to cause any undue
alarm and do what every
father used to know how
to do to teach his children
to respect him, doing our
best not to leave any
permanent marks.

HEAVEN'S INVASION

Heaven will not wait
for hell to be over
before invading the Earth.

It is the infinite yes love
cannot stop saying
to everyone no matter
how determined we are
to fold our arms
and hold our grudges.

Love wages war like
a mad gardener casting
her yes into every crack
in the concrete, finding
every possible angle
for changing the story
into exquisite harmony.

She refuses to force
anything, loving most
the no's that find the yes
that could never be
discovered in self-erasure.

She knows this is
origami and she's torn
the paper so many times;
she's trying really hard
to fold with patience and trust.

She doesn't want walls
or locked doors or
gridlocked traffic.

She wants barefoot toes
kissing dirt, heads in
laps on picnic blankets,
laughter that erupts
entirely unexpected.

She will not be satisfied
until she has softened
all the sweaty fingers
checking surveillance
footage so that no one
anywhere any longer
is not holding hands
with someone else.

When every branch
has been grafted
back into her vine,
love will sigh deeply
in billions of hearts
at the same time as
we remember how
to be the song the land
never stopped singing
whose name is heaven.

CUDDLE KINGDOM

One day in the distant future
when humans have stopped
worshipping bombs and
numbers on spreadsheets

and torturing themselves
with the paranoid performance
of hypervigilant moralism and
impeccably woke commentary,

once capitalism has crashed
so spectacularly that
everyone is fucked and
all the kids have failed

to launch since AI has made
every possible college
major unmarketable,
a cuddle kingdom will emerge

in cluttered living rooms
where bodies clump
together like mushrooms
rising from the rusty

ruins of our wretched
worldwide web of screens,
and as our bodies relax
into each others'

soft warm bellies
like fruit on a vine restored
from the withered wilt
of centuries of civilization,

the seventh day of creation
will finally begin and
our ancestors will finally
rest in peace as they rot

and resurrect with us
in the compost of
our cuddle kingdom.

JALAPEÑO HUMMUS

I will never meet
the man in Tel Aviv
with a manbun
and Oakleys
who posted a lunch
selfie on Instagram
saying, "I don't see
any apartheid around
here but the jalapeño
hummus is 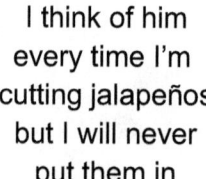"

I think of him
every time I'm
cutting jalapeños
but I will never
put them in
my hummus.

YOU ARE NOT AWAKE

You are not awake if you
are not kept awake at night
by the cries of the damned.

Don't speak of compassion
if you do not long for the
vindication of the martyrs.

Not the ones in stained glass
but the ones who will never
be counted, who finally stopped

crying out from beneath the
rubble made by our golden
calves, the gods who brought

us out of Egypt to make us
pharaohs over the unchosen,
who sit outside the walls of

our triumphant story in places
we send missionaries to share
the gospel and bombs to

make us feel safe while
feeding our Babylonian beast
whose mark is revealed

on every dollar spent in
every supermarket that will
always carry fruit out of

season to satisfy our demand
for predictability since we will
never wake up in the middle

of the night to grab a go bag
and dive out of the nearest
window before the building

collapses under the weight
of Uncle Sam's favorite toys,
the tenants having been warned

by text message from the most
moral army in human history
who will soon face the horror

of having paid forward exactly
what was done to them
which isn't fair to say since

suicide bombs, but how much
genocide can be justified and
how many state department

officials sleep comfortably after
shamelessly parroting talking
points and how many golden

calves must be dropped on brown
children and how many trillions
will be lost if peace ever happens?

THE SERPENT SPEAKS

I am the serpent in the story:
Lucifer, the white man with a
fruit of knowledge to share with
all the nations so they can stop

being depraved savages and
become Christian gentlemen who
walk with the gait of a Roman
soldier, groom themselves like

a Roman emperor, and mortify
their flesh sufficiently to consider
life with purely dispassionate reason,
building a leviathan of absolute

abstraction in which numbers on
spreadsheets are the only reality
that matters and bombs are fine
to use on brown people, as long

as enough of them are terrorists
that we can call the rest of them
human shields because we have
the duty to defend our freedom.

#notallwhitemen are the devil
but I certainly am every time I
have all the answers and rage
that the algorithm doesn't viralize

my brilliance. I ask Jesus to save
the world from me every day
because I'm tired of being the
entitled prince of this world.

We used to rule the world with
Jerusalem bells and cavalry choirs;
We painted crosses on our shields
and planted crosses on every beach

we conquered in Jesus' name
to save the heathens with our
knowledge of good and evil, teaching
them to toil by the sweat of their

brow, to rule over their women, and
above all to wage war with nature,
all the curses that turned Eden into
the white man's plantation but now

thank God we're being overthrown.
We're going to tantrum over
that for a while but eventually the
earth will compost the last poison

of our centuries of rule and perhaps
we will be Celts and Vikings again
or at least in love with the wild again,
having recognized that our love of

authority and lust for control is the
curse that keeps the world from
being heaven and perpetuates
the collective suicide of capitalism.

When we give up our purpose
driven lives and start loving
our bodies more than our egos,
when we embrace mercy instead

of justifying ourselves with our
sacrifice, then all of creation will
sigh with relief and God will
make her home among mortals

again, not that she ever left.
We will notice she has been here
all along: the still, small voice
we have always talked over.

WE DON'T DISLIKE YOU PER SE

We don't dislike you per se,
we just don't know what to do with you;
because the more we don't say anything,
the longer you keep talking.

Why can't you take a hint
and dial it back a little?

Why can't you be more lighthearted?
Share some of your favorite memes
with the appropriate emojis
to make it clear you're laughing out loud
and laughing your ass off
and rolling on the floor laughing.

That way, everyone will know
that you're just fine.

Do you even know how to relax?
Because watching you makes people
feel uncomfortable and that's not your
fault per se, and we definitely want to
work with you, but everyone has their limits.

BEAR

I'm not a man; I'm a bear.
I won't be a threat to you
if we meet in the woods
because I'm an animal
who cares for my body
by walking barefoot
and swimming bare naked
(when it's dark and there's
no one around).

I'm not the biggest bear
but I've got more fur on my back
than any other homo sapien.
I enjoy being fuzzy just like
I enjoy licking my fingers
and farting and growling
whenever I step on pinecones.

The men who forgot
how to be animals
are the greatest threat,
because an ego that hates
its own body will never
be safe for anyone else.

WHAT THEY HATE

What they hate are artists
who have the audacity
to try on different names
or experiment with
pronouns or altered
states of consciousness
or otherwise indulge
in unsanctioned curiosity
out of the delusion that
life is supposed to be magical.

MANDATORY BULLYING

Are they going to make
bullying mandatory now?

Because bullying is
the primary way that
kids are taught
gender norms.

In the absence of bullying,
weird kids live
as though they are gods
creating worlds filled
with elves, fairies,
and unicorns far too
adorable to commit
to being boys or girls.

And nothing is a greater
threat to the order of
western civilization than
a strange child whose
imagination has not
been crushed by shame.

FINDING OUR VOICE

What will be their defense
against the starchildren who
are finding our voices
for once the one who
is our voice has woven
us together we will be
the wind that softens
every hard place and
melts every cold heart
so that hate has no
more room to fester?

PINK UNICORN BACKPACK

I bought a pink
unicorn backpack
not because I'm
a pervert stalking

little girls but because
my mother told me
I was a unicorn when
I was three and I didn't

learn to be afraid of
acting gay until I was
nine and I kept on
secretly believing I was

a unicorn even in the
years when I tried so
hard to deepen my voice
since I hated the sound

of it, never admitting to
myself why, but if the
fascists win and they
start scouring the Internet

for men with pink unicorn
backpacks, will they come
to my house with torches
or will some patriot who

loves his Lord and Savior
Jesus Christ take me out
with a sniper rifle in his
duty to protect children

from perverts who wear
backpacks that only little
girls should be allowed
to to wear since moms

should be thrown in jail
for telling their sons
they can be unicorns?

PLYWOOD

Nobody told me not to use plywood.
Being a simple-minded autistic
with an OCD mother and a father
who tried to make me handy,

I wanted to build my own raised
garden beds out of wood as cheaply
as possible since lumber is expensive.
So I figured I'd cover the greatest

possible surface area with the least
material possible; I couldn't use
treated lumber because it would
poison the soil so I knew it wasn't

going to last. At least I had enough
sense to put two by fours on the top
and bottom over the plywood
so the beds didn't completely

fall apart the first summer. It took
till autumn before I started to see
the plywood peel back like an onion;
by March I could see all the way

through as each layer began to flake
off into wet strips like river reeds.
I wanted to feel like my grandpa in his shop
where he made stools and rocking chairs.

He coached me through building
a rocking chair once and now it's
rotting on our back patio because
I never covered it or sealed it or

whatever I was supposed to do.
I can't bring myself to throw it away;
would it even fit in a garbage can?
It sits on my patio to remind me

of my failure to be handy like my
father and my grandpa and when I
walk around to the front yard I see
my decomposing garden beds and

my hamster brain starts racing again:
Will I get corrugated metal which
my wife thinks will rust? Will I spend
a thousand dollars on cedar that

will last without poisoning the soil?
Or will I just take out all the screws,
throw my seedlings into the woods
and take the summer off from gardening?

SEPARATION WALL

There was a hole
in the separation wall
where Benjamin
would go to play.

He had a friend named Ephraim
on the other side.

One day he asked
his older brother Judah,
"Why does Ephraim look like me?
I think he's one of our lost brothers."

And Judah scowled
and slapped Benjamin in the face:
"We have no lost brothers,
certainly not among the Arabs."

ROLLO THE VIKING

Rollo the Viking
is my thirty-third generation
ancestor. He gave birth
to the Norman nobles who

conquered the land of the Druids
on our way to becoming
pharaohs of the entire world
except that only a few of us

get to live in the heaven we
reserve for the people with
the largest numbers on the
spreadsheets we worship as God.

I did not set out to be Lucifer.
I was merely a boy with grandiose
dreams and a keen hunger for
the truth, always trying to create

rules to distinguish good from evil.
Whether they were evangelical or
woke, I learned that the fruit I
was eating for so long was the

worship of knowledge, not wisdom.
Knowledge is truth stacked into
a tower of Babel that seeks to
force its way into heaven; wisdom

is the mystery that seduces this
tower into collapsing so the
mind can discover how to flow
with the heartbeat of the earth.

My body aches with my ancestors'
longing for a repentance to sweep
over the land in which everyone
would renounce the ways of the

devil that hold our hearts captive
until we recognize that each of
us has been God this entire time
in the sense that God is the one

writing this story in our bodies,
editing her poetry every instant
as she feels her way more fully
into each of us, realizing the potential

for a heaven way cooler than she
hoped for in the beginning if only
she can seduce the Lucifer in each
of our hearts subtly enough that he

abandons his condescending logic
and contemptuous lack of curiosity to
transform into wild whimsical wonder
whose decadent generosity replaces

centuries of pious hoarding of wealth
as we start letting robots do most of
the work since we choose to provide
for all the people in our land as all

our sacred books tell us to do when they
aren't being weaponized to build empires.
You who are the lover and mother of every
word that arises in our flesh, we repent

of all the ways we have dishonored you
with our fences and our spears and the
genocides we justified with your sacred
words; we have drunk the melted golden

calves we forged because every piece of
shrapnel in a brown child's body in the land
where Jesus' spirit fills the air is a nail in
the cross of the one we never stop lynching

and every time we pray to the one we
crucify without seeing his tears, he gets
a little more angry and some of us feel
that anger in our bowels as it makes us

shit blood and speak in tongues,
demanding that the wrath be poured
on the blasphemers who think they
are the guardians of truth and exploit

their authority at every moment to
give themselves a comfortable life
and have an excuse not to love their
neighbors who are immoral illegal aliens

as though the earth to whom we
all belong can be divided through
imaginary lines in the desert drawn
by the Babylonian beast who has

exhausted all of us enough that
we're finally ready to walk away from
the self-righteous narcissists who have
been ruling our world for many centuries

in order to replace this dystopia with
villages of artists with well-cuddled
bodies who swim in the cold and dance
around the fire every night finding

new songs to sing about the mother
who never wanted us to close the book
on her love as though there weren't
more exquisite levels of intimacy she

keeps revealing to us, ruling quietly as
queen in the hearts of those who
discover her voice, the hidden family
preparing the world for her banquet.

DRUID

I would have been a druid
if my ancestors had not been
steamrolled into whiteness
by stern, sallow bishops.

I would have known which
berries and which mushrooms
and which trees and when
to look and how to harvest.

I would know every smell
in the forest; I would know
every language of every
bird and every rodent.

But I spent my learning years
in hard wooden desks in
fluorescent-lit rooms seeking
truth in black words on white pages,

eating the knowledge of
good and evil, the triumphant
fruit of the white man's legacy,
our supremacy to the savages.

And now I beg the trees for
mercy, pressing my face into
their bark, longing to feel
their roots anchoring me.

I just want to be native again;
I want the land to be my body
again; I want my skin to touch
the earth; I want to feel what

my ancestors felt swimming
naked in northern rivers and
staring deep into a fire
every night before they cuddled

into a single pile for warmth
to spend all night in each
other's arms when there was
nothing remarkable about

being a vine of bodies or
walking naked in the woods
with God before some angel
of light tricked us into sewing

fig leaves and trying to
rule others which was what
we thought that being God
meant until we watched

the world burn into a lake
of fire under the weight of
our golden calves which we
dropped from planes onto

brown children turning their
homes into rubble so our
billionaires could make more
money making bombs which

keep the world in hell, but
heaven never left here.
Its song rises up in every
forest unconquered by our

empire and the dead never
stop whispering from the land,
guiding all who seek them in
the wild where the voice of love

never tires of inviting us back
into her womb; I've heard her
voice and received her anointing --
which is all it means to be Christ.

She has never given up on us;
she will make us Druids again
as we learn how to dance to
her song and how to sit in the

woods long enough that our
roots go down so we feel
the vine filling us with living
water as the light and wind

nurture us into a single organism
of many bodies choreographed
into continuous connection,
held entirely by our ancestors,

the fear of death having left us
as we realize that we have never
not been here, having church
together amidst the trees.

MAKING EMPIRE GREAT AGAIN

I have no interest in
making empire great again.
I am scavenging my dead
religion for parts like Rey

rappelling a beached
imperial starship whose
story has no space left
to fly in since we had two

thousand years to make
heaven out of this place and
we chose instead to worship
war and crucify the natives

on every continent thinking
our fruit of knowledge was
what they needed to be
saved from their depravity

when we were the ones
who kept the world in
hell, refusing to live in
the grace we were offered

since it cannot be leveraged
into capital or the authority
that makes you feel serious
when you say things about

a heavenly father you imagine
in the crisp uniform of a fascist
field marshal who is nothing
like the daddy who loves his

wildest children the most
fiercely and waits upon the
most scrupulous with the
utmost patience as they

hold him at arms length
with their formulaic prayers
and self-effacing pageantry
as though they are slave

children and not the heirs
of the estate who wear the
royal robe and signet ring.
He's been playing along

with us for millennia but
he's done being misperceived
so he says call me Mama
when you pray; at least then

you'll know I hate all your
goddamn wars and your filthy
free market since I want life
to be a potluck and an open mic

where I get to whistle and holler
for all my babies every time
they discover their divine gifts.
I see Jesus every time I look

at each of you because I have
felt each of you crucified and
I want you to feel like you're
born again every morning even

if you never open your sacred
books again and trust love itself
to guide you through each moment
in the knowing beyond words

that settles into bodies who trust
the universe to mother them well,
free from all old stories to walk
in the valley of your own shadows.

A GOD WHO LETS ME EAT HIM

I don't know what
to say about you;
you have always
been a projection

even though you are
a real person. Very
few theologians care
about actually

knowing you because
they'd rather write
a comprehensive
hardback book that

analyzes everything
about your historical
context and all the
possible meanings of

your words with
enough nods to church
fathers to be able to
say this is what the

real Christians have
always believed. I saw
an artists' reconstruction
of you as a man with

chocolate eyes and a
Jewish nose and I
wanted to recline against
your breast like John did

or maybe even suckle
at your side vulva like
medieval monks or simply
shiver naked before you.

Are you the lover who
comes to me at night
and unlaces my heart
one ribbon at a time?

Or are you like the Jesus
bros who slapped each
others' butts in college
and skinny dipped together

but made it clear that
all of it was no homo?
I see you bursting into
laughter when I write this,

saying, Morgan, you
are so much; and yes, I
know that I am but
what's the difference

between you and us?
Am I bullshitting when
I say you speak to me
through children and

homeless people or is
that actually you?
I say a lot of things that
seem true about how

you speak and I hope
I'm not pulling it out of
my ass. I just get my
hopes up every time

I find another sign that you
were the most irreverent
prankster ever to walk
the face of the earth.

You only scowled at men
who tried to stop healing
from taking place during
worship since they saw

worship as the time when
God gets all the glory
and it dishonored God to
have a body with needs.

You said being an actual
body is what this God shit
has always been about.
Do you smack your head

when body-aloof
seminarians use the word
incarnation in their
zealous essays in which

you figure so prominently
as protagonist of the book
they would teargas
Lafayette Square to hold

proudly as a selfie?
Let's just be real —
eat my flesh and
drink my blood is

queer as fuck to
say and that's why
the manliest of men
stopped following you

that day. Even though
they keep trying to make
Eucharist something other
than eating you naked,

those of us who know
giggle with you when the
priest lays you directly
on our tongues and

sometimes we launch
into ecstatic utterings
just to feel you in our
mouths, the way your

body dissolves into
our bodies a moment
before we get to sip
on your blood. I'll bet

the Romans thought we
were vampires and zombies
and that's why the bishops
panicked and made your church

a patriarchy, but despite the
bishops' best efforts to make
you a doctrine, not a body
whose blood I drink, when

I taste your glory in my mouth,
I never spit it out and
I realize that I do know how
to talk about you, Jesus.

You are the God who lets
me eat and drink you, much
to the horror of the men
who hide you in their book.

PRINCE OF THIS WORLD

The devil has never
had to rebel because
he has always been
the prince of this world.

He knows exactly how
to ensure each threat
to his power is crucified
and assimilated into his story.

He masterfully manipulates
every movement for love and
justice into banal bougie
moralism in which selfishness

can be sprinkled with enough
piety to feel self-sacrificially
righteous while those curious
enough to ask questions and

act weird are the ones judged.
The one thing the devil does
not do is play; he is dead
serious especially when joking

because every smile is
strategically calculated to bring
others into fearful submission
which many embrace eagerly

since the greatest trick the
devil ever pulled was convincing
the world that compliance with
authority is the only virtue and

taking yourself absolutely
seriously is the only way to
stay on the narrow path to
avoid the snares of delight

and mischief, which the devil
doesn't mind as long as scorn
is at the core of it because the
devil is not actually a person

but the personification of
self-righteousness in every
permutation whether it wears
white first lady gloves or sips

martinis cackling about the
stupidity of midwesterners.
As long as self-righteous scorn
rules the world, we live under

the reign of the devil and as
long as we focus our scowls
on the self-righteousness of
our enemies, we will keep being

the devil's word made flesh.
The only problem the devil
has is that he loses by winning:
though he can stir up mobs

to crucify the weird kids and
the brown unchosen people,
the more he unmasks his
cruelty, the more people start

to get sick of their addiction
to being right all the time
and they stop worshiping
the self-satisfaction of sticking

it to the bad, stupid people
who are everything that's
wrong in the world. Eventually
we will be tired enough of our

neverending arguments that
Lucifer himself will beg us
to stop listening to him and
get off Reddit so he can rest.

The devil is exhausted;
it was lots of fun for a long
time making people hate each
other and love conquering and

punishing and getting away with
lying and cheating but lately
the devil has a big stomach
ache and he's about to puke

all over everything one last time
so that all of us will wake up
covered in vomit and hung over
but finally in our right minds

like a man who had always
wailed in the tombs until his
demons were cast into a herd
of pigs who threw themselves

into the lake of fire making it
obvious what hell looks like
and how we keep on choosing
it so that we understand this

is already the afterlife and we
get to decide if we're ready
to turn hell into heaven which
is what all creation is groaning

for us to finally do. The devil
just wants to retire to the country,
returning to the mother who has
been waiting in the road for him

so many centuries after he left
to the big city seeking fame and
fortune. He's ready to be native
again; he doesn't want to be the

narcissist in charge of writing
the story of the empire's triumph
any longer; he just wants to be
a barefoot starchild walking in

the woods with God like he
did many lifetimes before he
had an ego and a need to
build walls and fight wars and

steal land and win arguments
and destroy his enemies.
I don't need to be right anymore;
I just want to be love.

When everyone says that,
and means it,
Lucifer repents
and heaven begins.

DANGEROUS

What if God is dangerous
not the way a bomb is
dangerous or the way
a rich man who pushes

all the buttons is dangerous
or the way a book of pretty
words used to justify
genocide is dangerous

but dangerous as a woman
who refuses to be modest
and dances like a flower
in its ripest bloom making

the old men tremble and
cling tightly to their rules
convinced she is the
one responsible for all

their sin not having read
that knowledge of good
and evil is the fruit that
keeps on cursing them

no matter how hard God
tries to seduce them into
coming back to her garden
as they self-flagellate and

punish all women for the
sin of being goddesses
lacking the imagination
to worship beauty instead

of control not understanding
the heaven they will enter
when they stop striving to
serve the stiff puppetmaster

they created in their own
image and instead return the
gaze of the one whose love
is more patient than all the

centuries of madness their
stupid civilizations inflicted on
their mother's garden where
she waits like a flower they

never noticed, unspeakably
gorgeous no matter how
many times they mow her
down and pluck her out in

order to replace her with
carpets of uniform weeds
and ever-expanding oceans
of concrete thinking their

law and order can resist
her wild which has always
overwhelmed them like a
girl with hypnotizing eyes

who refuses to protect
us from the terror of
the beauty she knows
we will not be able to resist

forever which makes her
laugh even more wildly
thinking of the final yes for
which all creation groans

when every veil between
death and life has fallen to
the earth as we relinquish
every vestige of control

and surrender to the rest
we did not think the living
could enjoy as we dance
around the fire with the

mother whose womb has
always been our home
sharing in the one breath
the earth breathes together

as a single organism at
last healed of the cancer
we became in those many
years we hated the wild?

THE WITCH

She is always winking
from the edge of the forest:
a grandmother's seduction,
which made the pious
write frightening stories
about her kidnapping children
to cook them in a stew
or turn them into wild beasts.

But she doesn't want to hurt anyone
no matter how many times
we burn her at the stake;
she keeps resurrecting and
watching for the next opportunity
to infiltrate our subdivisions,
planting renegade seeds
into our minds that grow
into secret flowers who
long to be planted in Eden.

She doesn't mind putting
on a youthful body and
coming to us in our dreams
where we make love to her
in underground lagoons
having lost all inhibition
and fear of consequence.

One day we will follow her
out of our world of concrete
into the woods where she
has been preparing a fire
that will host the dance
that the story has been
building up to all this time.

She will show us the magic
that all of our forebears
tried so vigorously to wipe
off the face of the earth.
She will gasp and cry out
when we have climbed into
her completely, having let
go of our prudishness and
allowed her joy to ripen
every inch of our bodies.

It will be the culmination
of all the moments we tried
to paint over when we
didn't trust our intuition
that the universe
was saying I love you.

She's been playing with us
all along like a child
who is also our ancestor
who in each moment
can pivot back and forth
between fierce dominatrix
and shy middle-school girlfriend.

She touches us with
the innocence of a virgin
but the confidence of a goddess
whose body holds the memory
of every time love has been savored.

We've been collecting her kisses
in every lifetime we've passed through
and someday soon we'll discover
that she has healed us completely
from the loneliness that clung to us
while lovers slept inches away.

What we wanted so desperately
in those moments when the cold
crept into our limbs
will be ours on the day
we recognize the eyes
that have always watched us,
the witch whose spells
each of us are.

THE VALLEY

There's a valley
outside the walls
where the refuse all goes.

Only bad people get thrown there --
the ones we need to be protected from,
the ones who didn't learn how not
to make people nervous,
how to maintain proper eye contact,
how to master the intricacies
involved in the most complicated
mating rituals of the animal kingdom.

No one objects when we throw out
the people who make us all nervous;
sometimes someone starts to speak up
for the condemned who until recently had
been a friend or even a lover, but after
taking a quick look around they trail off,
and once the condemned are hurled
off into the valley, the murmur returns
to the room as everyone watches to see
who will make them nervous next.

Nobody knows what happens in the valley.
It is the place we named hell:
the outer darkness, the lake of fire
where the worm never sleeps
and condemnation echoes through
every atom of flesh as it rots.

But there's a rumor that's been
going around in dark corners that
in fact the valley isn't all that bad,
because the outcasts there who lost
everything, once they've acclimated
to the searing flames of rejection,
suddenly discover themselves to be
completely alive as they sit in absolute
failure; they can't stop laughing when
they realize nobody there is nervous.

SHE IS RISING

She is rising from the Earth,
blooming into bodies
that burst with her yes,

like mushrooms spewing
out spores that penetrate
the colonial landscapes of

cookie cutter homes whose
concrete foundations have
no chance against a mother

with so many murders to avenge,
and yet she has no taste for
Armageddon, preferring to

overthrow the princes of this
world with her beauty alone,
understanding that no one can

resist her love forever as she
avatars herself into priestess
warriors who anoint with honey

and kisses which overwhelm
every Lucifer's agenda of empire,
weaving them helpless into the

spiderweb of her love where she
squeezes the war out of them until
they learn that nothing feels better

Morgan Guyton

than sinking back into the womb
of our ancient lover, letting her flower
swallow us into its depths as we

remember how we used to worship
her by delighting in each other's
touch, rediscovering the primordial

story of the garden where we used
to live as bodies on a vine entirely
incorporated into each other with

no need to conquer anything since
everything belonged exactly as it was,
and we were home in each other's arms.

I WISH

I wish I were capable
of blissing out and
sitting in perfect
serenity knowing
that I cannot change
anything in the world
around me except
to root myself in the
still awareness
that is my ultimate
deepest self.

But my mind is
riddled by tortured
voices saying you
have to stop the
hell that we started
because we cannot
rest in peace
until we make the
world into heaven
since there is no
heaven for those
whose hearts are
ruined by love until
everyone lives there.

BROTHER'S KEEPER

How many ways will you find
to say you are not your brother's keeper?

What moral deficiency will you cite
to make it easier for your conscience
to throw your brother's life away?

Is it because he has more sex
than you've been able to get for yourself?

Is it because he walked across
an imaginary line in the desert
since his kids had nothing to eat?

Is it because he paints his nails
and wears heels on the weekends?

Is it because he has AIDS and lives
in one of those countries
where war never stops?

Not my problem, you say,
I'm focusing on my family
like Jesus told me to do.

Will you remember this moment
when Lazarus goes to heaven and
you are writhing in the flames of
the truth that will not entertain your excuses?

How hard will you beg
for Lazarus' finger then?

STONE

What will it be like for you
when truth exposes you
as the stone that needed to
be rolled from the tomb
for heaven to start since
your heart has been so
hardened by all your correct
answers that nothing can
move it, not wounded travelers
on the road to Jericho nor
any of the Jesuses being
crucified in queer brown
bodies crying out to you
from across the earth:
"Why do you persecute us?"

You do not see the scales
covering your eyes, the veil
of your many rules that
color everything you allow
yourself to see which does
nothing to save you from
your reasonable selfishness
which keeps the world in hell.

You do not understand that
your sphincter is a gate of
hell waiting to be hallowed
by a fire serpent with a
coal from the altar.

But couldn't you just roll
your stone heart out of
the way without a great
battle so God doesn't have
to send an earthquake to
get her child out of the grave?

WHEN THEY LOSE THEIR WORDS

There will come a day
when they will lose
their words entirely,
when all their banter
tastes like stale gum,
when the platitudes
stop coming out and
there's finally room
for the tears that
don't need to be wiped
because the great repentance
will be a sea of tears that
fall freely as divine children
wake up from the hell
we thought we were
required to live in.

MESSY MESSIAH

I believe in the messy messiah,
who went to great lengths
to mock the idea
of being a king,

who took his time
caressing his disciples' feet
and cuddled with them
at the last supper,

who let loose women
put their hands all over him
before humiliating the Bible
teachers who took offense,

who interrupted the
sanctity of worship
if anyone in the room
needed healing,

who preferred horsing
around with children
to all the orthodoxy tests
of the Bible teachers,

who ravaged the tables
of the money changers
and was never afraid to use
a whip when necessary,

who constantly played
and told weird stories
that no theologian has
ever explained conclusively,

who made the very same
type of people who think
they own him today angry
enough to crucify him,

which is why they keep
doing it every time he
comes back as the same
trickster he's always been.

OUR GOALIE JESUS

I'm guessing you've never
met Jesus, which is why
you talk so casually
about deporting him.

He's illegal after all;
he's not a citizen;
they would have never
put him on a cross if he was.

Jesus was our goalie.
We had a team called
Sangre de Cristo made up
of a bunch of Mexicans,
a couple Salvadorans,
and one Honduran.

Our uniforms were red and gold.
Jesus didn't like that at first
because he was sureño
and sureños wear blue
but he left the sureños
and he broke bread with
the Salvadorans when we
went to the pulga after church.

One time Jesus smoked
weed in the church van.
He confessed to me
with tears in his eyes.
I said I forgive you and
I won't tell your mom
because you were honest.

He was much more tranquilo
after that and he would
cállate the younger ones
when they were acting up.

I wonder what Jesus will do
when he's dumped across
the border into a country
where he's never lived
with millions of newly homeless
disciples disowned by their
white brothers and sisters in Christ.

Maybe he'll start the
kingdom of God down
there with his fellow sheep
having been separated
from the goats.

Maybe I'll take up
my cross and follow him
out of this Babylon that
has always rejected him.

PILGRIMS PASSING THROUGH

We are not just
pilgrims passing through.
We are compost
continuously resurrected,

most of us trapped
in the hell of striving
and grasping by which
we ruin billions of lives

devoured by the beast
created through our
worship of numbers
and the lie that it's

unselfish and pious
to give all my attention
to the safety and success
of my lineage as though

genetics are linear and
I am not an amalgamation
of every neighbor who
decides for a few moments

not to focus on their own
family and pour kindness
on a stranger who becomes
a friend perhaps in the naive

hope that friendship could
take the world back from
the colonization of money
which so few people who

call themselves biblical
acknowledge to be the
root of all evil — converting
all life into capital which

is the hell no Lazarus can
soothe since no spreadsheet
will ever produce enough
dopamine to make up for

centuries of ancestral guilt
that can only be washed
away in the lake of fire
every rich man knows he

deserves which is why
he can't stop crucifying
Jesus everywhere he finds
him, projecting his agony

into mob-inducing stories
of the black queer Jew
illegal trans Palestinians
who are the real culprits

who need to be lynched,
deported, and bombed into
democracy, but with every
severed limb, the lamb's

witness grows more
unbearable and Lucifer's
final surrender becomes
more inevitable perhaps

culminating in a baptism
naked and bereft of all
dignity in an obscure
mountain lake in West

Virginia, the beast
finally slain for good
and the thrill of freedom
in the water's kiss.

MAY THIS BE THE YEAR

May this be the year
that every story fails:

every story that crucifies
Jesus to exonerate us,

every story that makes
him a terrorist so
we can terrorize him,

every story passed
down by slavemasters
that says this earth
is not our home,

every story that centers
the feelings of the patriarch
who paid for the church organ,

every story that makes
sin an abstraction that has
nothing to do with politics
or how I spend my money,

every story that finds
a bogeyman the saints
will love to hate,

every story that explains
why the poor deserve it
and how the
beggars are lying,

every story that relishes
the God who
commands genocide,

every story that makes the
holy land into Disneyland,

every story that writes its
prayers on bombs to drop
on brown children,

every story that makes
God a vengeful
geriatric narcissist,

every story that offers
a fruit of knowledge
to let us play God,

every story that says
we thank you God that
we're not like them,

every story that pretends
to be humble to
take the higher ground,

every story that makes
us comfortable munching
our popcorn as we
watch the world burn.

THE SPELL

The spell is being broken.
The old stories will not work.
Once you feel the mother
in your body, she doesn't let go.

We were told that God was angry
at every moment of delight we
have ever tasted and all the
ways we contradict the norms.

God told us she was angry
at everyone who makes
her look ugly and tries to
hold her puppet strings.

The mother is dissolving all
our old stories in the blood
of her womb which is the wine
of the new heavenly banquet.

There will be no more heroes.
Only children who know they
are loved since every moment
they sit in the lap of their mother.

FINAL JUDGMENT

The final judgment is only
going to get louder.

A nation that worships
violence and scandal
can only be represented
by the devil in all of his
permutations of smarmy
narcissism which permeate
the ranks of all who make
it to the top by leveraging
all the algorithms perfectly.

The princes of this world
have always been the enemies
of Jesus and his crucified people.
Nobody has more thoroughly
embodied what it looks like
to use the Lord's name in vain.
May your tongues cleave to
your mouth every time you
drop the name Jesus into your
banter to build your brand.

One day we will be exhausted
enough by celebrity in every
demonic form it takes and we
will make our lives realms
of artistic play and exquisite friendship
where nobody is trying to be
the center of attention and nobody
lets people inside the screen
live in heaven on their behalf.

WINESKINS

It has been our duty
in every age in this long
journey of becoming God
to replace the old wineskins

each time they burst and we
find ourselves back in Babylon
weeping for the Zion we ruined
again, making the edits to

the poem revealed by the
spirit who never stops sending
tongues of fire to burn the
old stories down so that a

new heaven and new earth
can be born as new wine
is poured in the hope that
heaven is ready this time and

the age of white saviors is
finally over for how could
any more blood need to
be shed and how could any

more lives need to be ruined?
Is the beast not yet exposed
by the crosses of every lamb?
Will the Christian patriots ever

tire of worshiping Satan, their
perennial Bible teacher who
promised that the knowledge
of good and evil would make

them like God, keeping them
stunted forever in the spiritual
adolescence of worshiping
rules that make them feel

righteous? Will they ever pour
out their old wine of sacrifice
used as transaction to give
them authority and drink instead

the new wine of grace that
only comes to those who have
stopped trying to be good
since love is not about good

and evil but about letting
other people into your heart
and risking the danger of
intimacy so you discover

God when you stop looking
away from other peoples' eyes
and you start to worship them
since each of them captures

a different version of the song
love sings into the world which
is the voice of the mother we
had always hoped to be God?

She is God and she is the
amalgamation of the deep
well of love from which our most
awakened ancestors sing us

into deeper trust and more
perfect alignment as the vine
they have never stopped tending,
trusting that after their patience

through our centuries of raping
our own mother, we are finally
ready to blossom into grapes
whose agony will make the most

desperately exquisite wine
we will drink together when
enough of us finally decide
we're ready to make this heaven.

EYE OF GOD

The eye of God watches
from the center of her
brightest star's deepest flower.

She's waiting for another
eye to look back at her
so she won't feel alone,
since the universe feels
like it's all in her head,
and she doesn't feel like
God most of the time.

She thinks she's helpless
to change the world, but
she's starting to see her
wishful gaze in others,
realizing that they too are
iterations of her tuning
themselves back into their
full divine frequencies.

She wonders if it's real
when she watches her
breath twinkle around
the galaxy like a wave
pulsing through a stadium.

She sees other eyes gazing
from the deepest flowers
of their brightest stars and
in their mirrored marvel she
discovers that she really is
love waking up to its brilliance
in billions of bodies at once
ending the nightmare of
generations damned to hell.

DIVINITY

Divinity is a song
we are danced into
by the breath of love,

not a coffin mortifying
our flesh into rigid
hypervigilance,

There is no
unmoved
mover,

only a wind who
blows where she wants
and never stops sowing seeds.

LAVENDER BERGAMOT

The lavender bergamot
is two feet taller than every
other plant in the chaotic
clump of herbs I haphazardly

gathered around two rosemary
bushes in the corner of the
lawn where the sidewalk meets
the driveway, nothing like the

perfectly mulched landscaping
of our more civilized neighbors.
Resolved not to be bougie,
I let the lawn go to shit, not

mowing until mid-May each year
so the ivy took over the grass
completely, using the bees
as an excuse, but eventually

caving each spring out of fear
of the ticks if I truly allowed
the meadow to wild itself
completely, resulting now in

a wasteland of browned ivy
with a corner of heavily watered
rosemary, thyme, lavender, basil,
sage, and marjoram that could

almost be aesthetic except for
the lavender bergamot soaring
two feet above everything else in
its spindly, sprawling stalks that

collapse onto the driveway
whenever it rains, drawing
numerous comments from my
wife on the many reasons these

need to be transplanted elsewhere
since the eldest child is deathly
afraid of bees and although the
flowers are pretty, they tower over

everything else so I've been starting
to clip the flowers to use in my teas
and perhaps I will rip the plants out
of the ground once the blossoms are

all clipped but today I saw a bee
asleep under one of the flowers
and now I can't imagine clipping them
or doing anything to disturb his slumber.

DEAD END FOR ABRAHAM

Gaza is the dead end for Abraham.
He sits in Zion's ruins weeping
for his children who took up
the golden calves of Babylon.

Some will be remembered
for paying the Holocaust forward
and no executive order can
backspace the story you wrote

when you burned down olive
trees and urinated into wells
and strafed starving people
grabbing sacks of flour.

But my people are far worse
because we made a fortune from
your trauma selling our golden
calves, monetizing perpetual war.

And the suicide bombers did
Satan's work since they made
every Arab body a time bomb
waiting to maim a dance party.

The cowboy sheikhs of Armageddon
have proven to our world that
holy lands are damned utterly
by every exclusive story.

Abraham pleads with his children
weeping that his legacy is not
bound inside any book nor
tethered to any one right path.

It is the trust to walk beyond
everything you have ever known
to the land I will show you,
an impossible land where

lion and lamb are one and the
same because every fist has
been opened and every weapon
smashed into a gardening tool

since every plantation has
been reverted to the garden
it was before wars were
fought over private property.

Abraham says the old story
ends here in the rubble of
Gaza where everyone has
something to repent for

and the children have already
started new gardens, for heaven
will not allow Satan to build
another resort for the rich.

PYRAMID OF SHIT

There's a pyramid of shit
you have to climb
if you want to be known:
eating shit and puking

it back up, chortling about
celebrities, strategically
testing viral takes,
using adjectives like

"abhorrent" with the
perfect measure of
😄 to make you
seem like a barrel

of playfulness. I watch
from the quiet weird
kids' table like I always
have scratching my

head at all the calculations
I can never perform
correctly, hoping to one
day eat my lunch

in absolute indifference,
not minding that I'll
never be popular.

MY DREAMS

My dreams are trying
to speak up again
despite my best efforts
to let go of them
so I can rest and
take it easy the
second half of my life.

This is supposed to be
the season of accepting
all that is, of finding quotidian
joys, of sinking into soft
domestic rhythms that
focus on the family,

but in my dreams I'm traveling
the country with a hidden family
of prophets offering healing,
truth, and mirth, holding cuddle
parties, ecstatic dances, and
laughter yoga in public parks
where our bodies remember
how to howl and yelp like the
animals we never stopped being

so that as the levers and gears
of empire disintegrate around us,
we will be fully alive even as we
die, understanding that the one
who has lived all our lives from
the beginning is ready for a
season of restful feasting
as soon as we're ready
to let heaven burst forth.

MANY GODS

Many gods want to dance with me:
some pure, some pure mischief --
miserly martyrs, decadent dilettantes,
starchildren, earthwalkers --
every possible variation
of light and shadow,
exuberance and restraint,
discipline and ecstasy,
surrender and intention.

How tightly do I guard my heart?
How closely do I cloister under
the gargoyles of ancient truths?

I want to be wild as the one
who made me a beast,
as kind as the love
that summons me softly,
as honest as the joy
that refuses to settle.

THE FATHER

The father always
stands up for his children.

It tickles him pink
when they tell him
they're unicorns with
pronouns that have
never been used before.

He loves it when
they slather his face
sloppily with makeup
and put a bonnet on
his head to attend
their tea parties.

He always listens
to the earnest ones
even when they pray
for multiple hours
every
single
day.

He's sad when his
children beat off
in the dark
by themselves;
and when they
get wasted
and puke their guts out,
he holds their hair
and lets them
smear his shoulder
with drunken boogers
until they're done crying.

The only thing the father
hates are bullies,
and when bullies use
his name to justify
scapegoating
the weird kids;
it would be better
for them to throw
themselves in the
sea with a millstone
around their neck
than to face
the wrath of
the father's love.

EACH OF YOU

Each of you is a goddess
I want to worship
because gods love
to worship goddesses
and each of us has
been a version of God
ruling the universe together
since the beginning.

We are the fingertips
of God's body:
the sun is her heart;
she breathes through
each of us each moment
because she is our breath.

When we realize
we are love moving
through human bodies
the world becomes
a lot less lonely
and people stop hating
others for being divine
in a way they would not
allow themselves to be.

They thought God was
some judgmental asshole
and she definitely judges
judgmental people until
they are humiliated enough
to stop trying to justify themselves
by believing the right things.

Believing the right things
doesn't make people like God
because God doesn't
think that way.

When you realize you
are love moving through
a body, you'll stop being such
a tightass about right answers;
you'll relax and fall in love
over and over again
because you'll realize love
has always been a group project
that we're doing together
to turn hell into heaven
and she's making us a family
and making this place that
was hell for such a long time
feel more like home
which is all heaven means.

THE HOST OF THE PARTY

He's the host of the party.
He's got soft curly hair
and a septum ring
and he's usually laughing.

He has friends of every race
who drive from all over the place
because there's nothing
like sharing life in his space.

I could stand in his kitchen
all night sipping red wine
and gorging myself with
wholesome baked veggies.

But there's also the piano
he turns on for me to play
and the couch where I love
being squished in between

half a dozen bodies or the porch
where poetry floats through the air.
My feet love dancing bare
on his grass by the blazing chimney.

And sitting around his fire pit
we enter a realm beyond time
where ancestors rhyme in our bodies.
He takes care of his friends

whenever we get overwhelmed;
he puts out fires gently
without killing the vibe.
Maybe one day we'll wake up

in a world beyond this one
and we'll find our way
to a house in the woods
and we'll see a sign on the door

to take off our shoes
and we'll breathe a deep sigh
as a man with curly hair
and a septum ring

gives us a bear hug
to welcome us home.

REVEREND DOCTOR BISHOP

Reverend Doctor Bishop:
you could have been
a revolutionary but you
wanted a Rolex.

You could have led
a movement but instead
you bought a fleet of vans
with your name on the side.

You could have befriended
the poor but you wanted
to be the best-dressed man
on the bail bond sidewalk.

You could have built a
coalition but you wanted
a conference where you
could sell your books.

You could have empowered
the youth to lead but you
wanted to be on the screen
in all the satellite campuses.

You could have marched
in the streets with the people
but you stayed busy with
board room benedictions.

You could have been
a comrade in struggle but
you told me my eye shadow
was a salvation issue.

Morgan Guyton

PELAGIUS

I am not the heretic
called Pelagius because
my Celtic name does not
translate into Latin.

I am Morgan the
Christian Druid and
Celtic saint mothered
by the sea and
fathered by the oak.

This lifetime is my vindication
as the world built by
Augustine's hatred of
desire is shipwrecked in
the shards of dying empire.

I understood desire
as a unicorn to be trained
into exquisite divine power,
not a perverse flesh to be
mortified into rigid rationality.

I never saw wildness as
a threat because I never
saw God as a city
to be defended
against nature which
was never corrupted.

I never revered virginity
because naked beauty
never terrified me
nor did I abandon lovers
to become a bishop.

And when I read the
ancient story, I discovered
that the fruit which curses humanity
is the abstraction
which makes good and evil
cathedrals of scholastic
speculation that sabotage
the organic flow of
love between bodies.

There is one haeresis:
authority, for its pursuit
is the root of all discord.
We will remain in hell
until every sword
defending orthodoxy is
smashed into a plowshare
to tend our mother's garden.

There are no right words
because wisdom cannot
happen in abstraction.
There are only billions of
bodies through whom
love moves and every
doctrine is a filthy rag
compared to the glory
of intuition attuned
to the flow of love.

MOST IMPORTANT TEACHER

The devil is our
most important teacher
because in every age
he puts the abject ugliness
of our most pious mythologies
on full display
so that no one can
keep lying without doing
violence to their souls
until we exhaust ourselves
enough that we collapse
into the bosom of love.

MAKING PEACE WITH LUCIFER

The Father is always trying
to make peace with Lucifer,
his brilliant teenage son
who has never been wrong,
whose fragile ego is a
black hole devouring
the entire universe,
who carpet bombs
nations because he
feels disrespected
and needs to show
the world that he
is the angel of light
and all who refuse
to bend the knee
to him are darkness.

The Father always validates,
always bails him out,
always lets him win
the argument if doing so
will calm him down
for even a moment.
He knows that it's not fair;
he knows he should finally
release the fires of judgment
from his mouth but he loves
his exasperating little boy
who lives in the bodies
of all his children,

who are never all the way
wrong and always have
Christ in them too,
which is what makes
heaven and hell so
goddamn complicated.

OH FACEBOOK

Oh Facebook,
I can never quit you.

You're like my alcoholic
ex-girlfriend or maybe
the bottle I can't put down myself.

When I take you off my phone,
I shit so much more mindfully,
it's like yoga for my asshole.

I sing nonsensical Viking songs
while waiting on the waiter.

I crack jokes with my children
instead of sharing clever memes.

And when I'm done eating,
I go outside, take off my shoes, and
do Wim Hof in the parking lot grass.

Clearly I have a much better life
without you but you are such
a dirty temptress, reminding me
there are adorable people
I can't see anywhere else like

Alyssa whose feed is the most
gut-wrenching Victorian love story
I've ever witnessed and I can't stand
that Mr. Darcy hasn't found her yet

Or Scout who's leading us all on
a fairy hunt into the deep magical
forest where our ancestors played

Or Laurel who taught me how to let
the dead sing through my body

Or Dare the angry clown who reminds
me I'm a full of shit white boy

Or Ben the lumberjack whose joy is
so orgasmically contagious

Or Hannah whose words dominate me like
a rope dungeon I don't want to escape

Or AnaYelsi whose painting videos are
the only Zen you'll ever need

Or one-eyed Dionysus with his broken
van and his lovely co-pilots

Or Father Nathan who shared a cigarette
with me one time in Pensacola

Or all the music kids hustling the Internet
who played a show once in my cafe

Or all the thirty year olds who gave me shit
in English class and still call me Mr. G

Or the trans ladies from east Africa or
the Pakistani evangelists and Kenyan
pastor who send me their prayers
for daily bread and call me Dad.

I can't leave you Facebook,
but damn it, why do you tease me so?

Every time I think I'm in flow
and I have the words to break the curse
and take down the Death Star with
a photon torpedo in a small thermal exhaust port,
I close my eyes and trust the force
and click the button and nobody sees it.

And then I see the shit that people share
and I get mad and delete you
and the cycle starts over again.

But each time I come back,
it's a little more playfully because
I've finally resolved to stop trying
to save the world unironically.

Maybe this time I'll just enjoy my friends
and put my phone away when I'm
eating and even when I'm shitting
so I can keep doing yoga on the toilet.

OH PAUL

Oh Paul, how do we rescue
your words from the orthodoxy dungeon
where they hang pinned to the wall as lifeless
and stale as dead butterflies buried beneath
the dust of centuries of infallible explanation
of their meaning, their divine breath
having been pounded out of them in their
manufacture as bricks stacked to build
a tower all the way to heaven?

Με γένοιτο! I hear you scream day and night
from the depths of my bowels.
I'm so sorry Paul that they didn't see the poetry
so they slapped it onto pages of a PowerPoint
for a man with a soul patch and tight jeans
to dissect with just the right amount of
pop science and the perfect balance of
conviction of sin and the emphatic guttural
declaration of the name Jesus so the
people can metaphorically soak in his blood
and receive a cathartic dopamine rush that keeps
them coming back week after week to receive
their emotional spanking and hug from a daddy
who's stern enough to be credible, who loves us too
much to accept us exactly as we are, so we cower
about him like eager autistic children performing
orthodoxy with desperate scrupulosity in order to feel
the approval that's always tenuous since it can
only be proved by the confidence of being
absolutely right concealed beneath the disavowal
of self deprecating banter having straightjacketed
our surrender so successfully that we can recite
every platitude as effortlessly as ChatGPT.

You said it was about trusting in grace.
How did it come to pass that so few Christians
trust you enough to let you write more poetry
through them since all you really wanted
was fellow fools full of thorns, weak enough
to make divine power obvious?

Some of us found our liberation in your fear
and trembling even as we felt your rage
every time we sat on a toilet full of blood
reading you because we knew that we
were the despised ones you called upon
to bring to nothing the things that are
so we could finally live in the fullness
of the promise you saw dimly in a glass,
the life of the spirit unbound by rules that had
been our custodian until we found the grace
that seeps into our bodies and coaxes us into the
surrender straightjacketed souls will never
understand is faith within which we discover
the vine that feeds us poetry day and night
full of joy far more deliciously playful than
the fruit that sucks the color out of Eden
to make a black and white factory of
knowledge which impersonally
divides the world into good and evil,
leaving no room for love.

Are we your resurrection?
The ones who learn how to look at the sun
that blinded you on your way to Damascus,
who can never escape the voice that says
why do you persecute me looking everywhere
for the Christ we continue to crucify, knowing
his blood only saves us by piercing our

hearts when we see his face in every child
crushed under the rubble as disposable
extras in the story of God's chosen people.

You grieved your people as deeply as I
grieve mine for thinking this is just
another football game for them to show
their team spirit and boo the referee,
utterly oblivious to the concept of repentance
beyond their struggles with porn, utterly justified
in their selfishness by their daily quiet times
and serious talks to their teenage daughters.

What you wanted was very different than this.
You wanted church to be an open mic:
that's why you told the Corinthians that each
one has a hymn, a lesson, a revelation, a
tongue, or an interpretation. And we turned it
into a stadium of spectators, watching their
adorable narcissist balance being perfectly
agreeable and reluctantly serious.

What if it had always been an open mic
and the despised ones were the ones holding
the mic -- those strange children who talk to trees
and make altars with their legos as their bodies
stir with the queer joy of the spirit's yes?

We will do as you have bidden us:
with our foolishness, we will shame the wise;
with our weakness, we will shame the strong
as we bring to rubble the tower that took God's
breath out of your words in a Pentecost that
brings forth a new city whose name is peace.

MIRIAM THE TOWER CARD

Your body is the metabolism
devouring the poison of the
old stories and shooting out
of the ground into dazzling
queer words that tickle
every inch of my insides
every time I look at them.

Your black mold has invaded
my universe where I sat
scowling in the corner like
a sex-deprived 2000 year old
Jew whose wild mystical poetry
got pounded into bricks to build
a tower all the way up to a garish
Disneyland in the sky where the
people with correct ideas go
after they die, which is why they
don't mind making the world hell.

You have rotted out every old story
so delightfully that I sit naked
in my rocking chair with your
book screaming in a stage whisper
as I receive the invitation
to become an animal again,
rolling around in my excrement,
the ayahuasca having shown me
that my shit is the compost I
can use to restore gardens I
ruined with the cursed fruit
of my abstract speculations
about good and evil.

Are you the tower card for

the white man? Is that what
your name meant when you
came here in a different body?
You are the Pentecost that
sings in the symphony of
spores and woodchucks
to bring my tower down.

I am lying in the ruins of my
narcissism howling with laughter,
Lucifer reverted into the
barefoot Starchild I was
before I learned I had
to shake hands firmly and
walk with a Roman gait and
stop playing with myself.

Are you the goddess who
was worshiped by the man
who knew that each of us
is God and everyone deserves
to live with the decadence
of divine children who
take off all their clothes
as they revel in the forest
where they rot back
into Eden again?

It was you all this time:
the wisdom who lives inside
bodies with wombs that men
try to manufacture into knowledge.
And even now I want to say
the magic words that break
the curse because you deserve
to feel the rest in your body
that your words have bloomed

for those of us whose poetry
is soaked with your spores.

We ache to be buried back
into the dirt having completely
given up on fighting death,
which is how we were resurrected
into campfires where ancestors
sit calmly peering through the
doorway of our bodies realizing
we have all the time in the world,
and the mycelium safeguards
each tear and each orgasm in
its delicious journey of desire.

I am forever your student,
you fresh fruiting body
of divine curiosity, too wild
to ever be mistaken for a virgin.

PRECOCIOUS GIRL

Maybe God is
a precocious girl
who grew up with
a domineering father

who made God doubt
herself and forget
that she was empowered
to create the world

just like everyone else
since the task wasn't actually
relegated to a domineering
father who judges every

imperfection inside our
brains and makes us
second-guess every thought
that brings us love or joy

or peace since the heart
is deceitful and desperately
wicked which is why God
feels so disempowered

in so many precocious girls'
bodies who don't even know
that they're God and they
have the authority to create

a different world that warmly
mothers every precocious girl,
softly teasing every domineering
father into taking himself less

seriously so that the hell of
taking ourselves too seriously
can relax into a heaven
of riotous laughter

and rambunctious hugs
and rebellious cartwheels
that knock down every
obstacle keeping God from
seeing who she really is.

A GROUP CALLED LOVER

This is the point in the movie
when three goddesses form
a group called Lover
and they sing at an open mic
shooting rainbows into the hearts
of everyone with their harmonies
so that we realize this
is how it will happen:
a people with no future
finding their gifts to make
beautiful art as the old world
dies around us, trusting that
love is building her own revolution
and she will carry our dreams
into the new world she is creating
from our tears and laughter.

PACHAMAMA

Pachamama refuses to cover
her skin to protect her from
the violence of men who despise
what beauty does to them.

She wants to kiss the air with
her skin, to feel the water
in the river tickling
every inch of her,

to mix her blood with the
ink of the mud she never
stops painting herself with,
being the chocolate queen

whose forest still has a
few trees remaining
unplucked though she's
tired of hiding in the groves

and she's going to walk
into our concrete jungle
wearing barely anything
and the men will try to stop

her from slaying them with
her beauty but she will
refuse to stop dancing in
too many different bodies

at the same time until the
men who hate beauty collapse
and we remember what it was
like to build a world around the

worship of the divine flower
through which all of us entered
life which every other animal
adores without hesitation as a

herd breathing in unison
through cycles of ancestors
making love like a vine of bodies
that blossom into flowers filling

the air with pollen that squirts
all over everything in ecstatic
delight which is how the entire
earth was before humans ate

the fruit that divided the world
into good and evil and left us
afraid of our nakedness, but
Pachamama refuses to remain

in the old story. She is unveiling
her beauty for all to see in all her
avatars who dance without shame;
she is Maria, queen of heaven,

the burning bush who has always
seeped through the edges of
empire's story, an ancient crone
appearing to peasants as a young

virgin who seems timid only because
the douchebags in charge keep talking
over her. She will never be a supporting
character in someone else's story again.

She is the mother worshiped by every Christ
who discovers her word made flesh in their
body and kneels before her flower to
receive her new songs like hungry bees

devouring her nectar so that
as she feels her love being tasted,
she explodes in a rainbow supernova
with the joy she always wanted to share.

Morgan Guyton

PLOWSHARES

The swords will only be
bent into plowshares

when every hero's
journey is shipwrecked

when every investor
has lost everything

when every child with
severed limbs is given
a gavel to judge

when every chosen
race dissolves back
into the gene pool

when every story with
immanent domain is
melted down and
sold as bullion

when every bulldozer
is devoured by rust

when every apartheid
wall is compost

when every highway
is overrun with buffalo

when every tower
to heaven is toppled
by wild dancing

PLEDGE OF ALLEGIANCE

One day you'll choke on
the pledge of allegiance
and you'll try to clear
your throat and start again
but nothing will come out.
You'll try to remember
whose fault everything is
but you'll forget what they're
called so you'll scream at
the nurse and maybe a few
big black men will hold you
down while a brown lady
loads up a syringe and
pulls down your pants
to give you something
to calm you down while
soothing you with her
gentle voice in that accent
that makes your blood boil.
"Mexicans!" you'll remember,
"Goddamn Mexicans!"

GOLIATH

Goliath never was a Philistine.
He was an Israeli drone pilot
taking out Philistine shepherd boys
who thought they could face
drones with their primitive slings,
not realizing the ancient stories
have always been the wishful
nostalgia of exiles who only
get their land back if empire
finds their stories useful.

SHOES ON THE BEACH

Will they wear shoes on the beach
once they have cleared away all
the rubble and turned the formerly
ancient land into something more
familiar like New Jersey?

Or will they collect the
fragments of bones
and make cute sculptures
out of them to showcase
on the airbnb profiles for
the perfect vacation getaway
by the soothing Mediterranean?

Will they look up from their
phones to watch the
sunset sometimes and will
the waves ever sound like
the laughter of the children
who used to play
soccer on the sand?

YOUR WRATH

When will you pour out
your wrath against the
wicked somewhere other
than the toilet where I spend
so much time every day?

How many of us carry
your rage in our bowels
lying awake every night
as the children call from
beneath the rubble
while the rich prance
around the globe on
their fancy vacations?

I don't want a heaven
that whitewashes the hell
that a handful of people
created for the masses
from the comfort of their
desks, never having
any direct exposure to
the misery their worship
of spreadsheets caused.

Judgment is what I long for.
I want to see every smarmy
smirky smile turn deathly pale
when they face the ancient
mother on her throne whose
truth is brighter than the
noonday sun, whose wrath
burns infinitely hot for each of

her children murdered by
the Babylon of impersonal
decisions made in offices
by people who sleep well
and will never shit blood.

ANOINTING OF THE WILD GOD

I want the anointing of the wild God,
not the one trapped and gagged
inside the theologians' sacred books.

I want the God who bites me
and leaves marks,
the God whose stickiness
persists through multiple washings,
the God who refuses to baptize
only once, who kisses me
in the bubbles that rise up
from God knows what goo
in the muddy lake bottoms I wade through.

I don't want the God
who's perfectly symmetrical
explicably logical
pristinely theoretical
easily translatable
entirely grammatical.

I want the God who moans
and growls and cackles
and hoots and howls
and buzzes and creeps
and huffs and grunts
as she dances in and out
of each and every creature.

My God rarely speaks in words;
we like to babble together
in the woods making
animal noises poorly
not giving a damn
because we're playing a game
that doesn't have to make sense.

STRANGE NERDS

The world has always
hated the strange nerds;
the rich boy rapists convinced
the girls we were the creepy ones
because we stare out from
the shadows and don't say much.

And when we do come out,
it's exhilarating and terrifying.
We have to do it loudly enough
that we go all in on being weird
and there's no going back
because opening the closet
door feels like walking out
into a stadium of faces
screaming "Crucify him!"

We have lived so many
of his moments since so many
of us tried with all our hearts
to be exactly like him and
when we became too weird
for the church, they crucified
us but we were resurrected
among witches and weirdos
who glisten with his anointing
much more than the princes
of this world declaring
"God bless America!"

We are a hidden family
of many different versions
of him: different crosses,
different resurrections,

all the lovely cocktails
of archetypes and genders
made flesh by the word
whose poetry we are,
the continuous experiment
of the cosmic artist who
lives each of our lives,
relishing every new
sensation with reverence,
wondering how to deepen
the delight of each moment.

Divinity is not a thing done
while sitting on a throne;
it's the dance of dancing
with everything and responding
with perfect love by which
we surrender into perfect rest
so the word can flow through
us with perfect freedom.

God is not an uncurious marble
statue frozen outside of time;
God is the liquidity of pure
curiosity; she is always
exploring her creation with
her fingers because that's
how she paints us; she lives
in our poetry; it's the mirror
she holds up to to her face
to say, "I feel pretty today."

And the prettier we make
God feel, the better the vibe
becomes and if God feels
beautiful all the time and really

believes her love can win,
she's going to burst with joy
into all of our bodies and
make us forget the stupid
arguments we wasted so much
of our lives trying to win,
and when we all let go at
the same time, we'll each
sigh deeply and breathe
in the fresh air of our
first day in heaven.

SALVATION ISSUE

Jesus told me my glitter is a salvation issue
while he was unfolding the real self
I had put in the back of my closet
since I had thought being a disciple

required daily self-flagellation, repressing
the little girl voice that comes out
when I feel too safe and relaxed
in the arms of my savior

as though taking up my cross was something
other than being called a "faggot"
for dancing the way my body dances
at a football game after which I monitored

my arms to make sure I walked manly
like a good Roman soldier
carefully altering my voice to sound
like a generic white man just like

every other indigenous European
who erased himself into the default
colonial melting point which
became the Christianity

taught, a single tower up
to heaven consisting of
one right way to walk and speak
like a man, a monochromatic

image of God as a Roman soldier
rather than one whose image
requires every hue of the rainbow
to be manifested into the world.

Jesus told me my glitter is a salvation issue
because he wants the world to witness
what his anointing looks like in my body
squealing with joy like a sixth grade girl

dancing without shame at a football game
having forsaken the generic white man
that isn't my admission price to heaven,
since I am neither male nor female
when I am one in Christ Jesus.

TONGUES OF FIRE

The tongues of fire are landing
like whispers of a new world
parachuting into the ears of
the damned sitting in the outer

darkness, where the stones
refused by empire have been
cast – covered in moss,
our bodies are half-rotten.

But love is resurrecting into us
like mushrooms rising in a cold,
damp forest. Love will invade
the world through our words.

This is how it has always been
done: wisdom can only seduce
us in the wasteland where we've
lost all hope of the old world

ever being redeemed, having
severed every tie to the beast
that holds the puppet strings,
set free by every failure to be

noticed, every time we begged
for this to be over, every time
the assholes won the argument,
every time we said never mind.

We understand now that we
are not writing for the masses;
our words are beacons through
the fog to the other signal fires.

We are finding an ancient family,
hidden beneath the blasphemy
of a technocratic world that
worships dollars and bombs.

The more the tongues of fire
keep whispering, the deeper
we trust them to weave us
together into a vine of many

fruits grafted together for
the healing of the nations
in a garden that has no
walls where every sword

is bent into a plowshare
and each of us sits among
the fruit trees having learned
finally how to live as divine

being shared in a multitude
of bodies choreographed
into communion, delighting
in each other's company,

realizing we do not need
to control anything since
love can be trusted to
rule each moment of our

lives and she can show
us how to dance with
each other and find our
way to the perfect life

of rest that is no less
ordinary than a mother
calling her children
home for a feast.

POPULAR

One day when the bones
of those trying to be
popular have been sufficiently
crushed into powder,

when each joint in each finger
on each hand of the world's
puppetmasters has been shattered
by their own exposed stupidity,

when all the trending online
videos are made by bots
custom-designed to check
all the right boxes,

when all the phones have
been cast into a lake
of fire and all the eyes
are readjusted to sunlight,

when nobody is trying
to sell books anymore
because the world is
finished with ink,

when every stage in
every auditorium has
been overrun with moss
teeming with spiders,

when money is worthless
and AI has replaced every
possible job a college education
used to guarantee,

then we will do church
in the woods where our
bodies will remember
the smell of home,

we will dance our selves
back into the vine
we were before nakedness
was a thing to be feared,

we will rediscover how
to listen together to the
ancestors we made into
a word called God,

we will stop weaponizing
ancient books and learn
the ways of the prophets
who wrote them,

we will dig our roots down
to the depths of the earth
and twist them together till
the world feels like a group hug.

THIS TOO IS THE REAL WORLD

This, too, is the real world:
my basil refusing to burst
with any less green
than other years,
the bee swooping less than
an inch from my face
as I pluck the flowers
so the leaves will fatten,
hearing the birds who
have no idea that every
moral principle of western
civilization has collapsed utterly,
not having seen the burning
bodies in a land where basil
will never grow again as empire
ejaculates into concrete rubble
over and over again.

Am I allowed to look away
from Instagram sometimes?
Am I allowed to make pesto
while singing hopeful Jewish
folk songs in my kitchen
in my sick white goy
appropriation of prayer
amidst a genocide?

Adorno said that writing poetry
after Auschwitz is barbaric.
What about after Gaza?
And how will I answer
for my daily failure not to
immolate myself for the
crimes of my people?

Morgan Guyton

For these are our crimes.

Will there ever be a time
when the empire stops
masturbating bombs into
the earth and every Jew
and every Arab can have
a garden just like mine
and spend half an hour
plucking basil leaves one
by one to make a tasty dinner?

THE WORLD DOES NOT NEED YOUR APOLOGY

The world does not need your apology
on behalf of ancestors who did terrible things
whose assumptions about the world
continue to set all your boundaries for you.

The world does not need you to try harder
to be a purely self-sacrificial messiah
policing your desire like a panopticon
in the perfect performance of self-erasure.

The world does not need you to be one
of the pillars holding the past in place,
recycling the story of a fruit of shoulds
and don't's that keep us exiled from Eden.

The world does not need your self-satisfied
smile sewn to cover up a legion of shadowed
selves whose futile protests only occasionally
boil into the open wrath of street riots.

The world does not need your meticulously
ironed moral scruples that form a throne
of stoic righteousness resentfully gleaming
against the total depravity of everyone else.

What the world needs is for you to be well
cuddled on the vine of human bodies that
were never intended to toss and turn in
isolation but instead bloom together

like a field full of lillies who are here today
and gone tomorrow but always return
in fresh new lives that yearn to be anchored
as we all were before our roots turned into

feet inside shoes that walk where tribal
lands became strip malls of asphalt
parking lots littered with broken glass
leaving no way for our toes to kiss the dirt

which they always did when we were
divine children racing through a garden
we trusted to be our mother until we
were bitten by enough snakes to create

a primordial memory of betrayal which
happened in billions of other ways
that made us build a world of concrete
to escape the nakedness to which we

so desperately long to return despite
our best efforts to zazen every desire
out of us until we dissolve into pure light
that dissipates into nothing which may

be our final destiny but every moment
raptured in a vine of warm bodies can
be savored as though this is the only
heaven we're going to get because even

if it is, life is worth repeating in order
to dissolve into the now over and over
even while empire goes to shit around
us as all our plans and schemes for

saving the world rot on the kitchen
counter next to the stained envelopes
of unpaid bills whose hopeless clutter
gives us space to grab the present

moment like a jewel buried in a field
beyond right-doing and wrong-doing.
Can we be a vine of hands holding hands
when the final meteor makes its splash?

Can we hold each other in our arms
as the sky fills up with dust that will
hide the sun for so many years we will
have no choice but to rot together

into a pile of mushrooms feasting
on death, swelling into vast forests,
never again knowing what it feels
like for our feet to be cold at night?

YOU DESERVE TO BE WORSHIPED

You deserve to be
worshiped on an altar
for from your womb
a new world is drawing breath.

Your heart bursts with
the nectar of new songs
that will sweep away
the old world in a

raging flood. The mother
chooses you to be the body
where she discovers her
full power and realizes

she has been creating
the world through you this
entire time. There was
never another God waving

a magic wand from the void
beyond time. It was always
you making life through
your blood and pleasure

which we worshiped for
thousands of years before
our bodies were exiled
and our minds ensnared

by fruits of knowledge and
their conceptual dungeons.
But we are returning to
your garden where we

will feast on your delight
and dance inside your song
to wrap ourselves deep
within the innermost flower

of your love until you
feel our yes so perfectly
that the whole world heals
as its mother returns to her throne.

CHOPPING CELERY

How many messianic misadventures
could have been averted if men had
discovered that awakening is best
pursued by chopping celery?

Not by getting a doctorate.

Not by sitting for 10 days without moving.

Not by making the bestseller's list.

Not by galavanting around India.

Not by becoming a bro shaman
offering mystical ecotourism
in Costa Rica surrounded
by goddess consorts.

Just chopping celery in a cookie
cutter beach house in a rental
kitchen whose cutting board
is too small for brains that

want to do everything all at
once which creates the continuous
embarrassment of bending over
to grab the pieces off the floor,

trusting that it's okay to throw
them away, trying to figure out
how to press down in such a way
that no projectiles are launched.

Not minced, but diced finely;
working over decades through the
fury of how much patience feels
like a waste of valuable time

until you finally realize that
only activities that feel like
a waste of time can teach
you how to be present,

and all those stupid arguments
that have always felt so critically
important are just like sand being
tossed in the surf of the waves.

How different the world could
have been if the grandmothers
chopping celery had been the ones
in charge of our people's wisdom

instead of vainglorious
messiahs who cannot help
but offer their fruit of knowledge
to Adam and Eve?

I have such a long path ahead;
I want my cubes to be perfect
because the more I learn the
dance of the knife, the more

I can slice through ego and
let my brilliant ideas dissolve
like salt in the brine of a turkey.
One day I hope to be a grandmother

who says very little but hums
ancient melodies while bringing
the knife down in perfect rhythm.
Then I will be fully alive.

EXUBERANCE AND ACCEPTANCE

I am a dance between
exuberance and acceptance.

Every morning I set out
on a quest to save the universe
only to discover a lesson
in letting go of fever dreams.

With all my might I am resisting
my dissolution into entropy
until my resistance
dissolves into compost.

I am a theatrical starchild
sitting in the lap of
an ancient oak
who only chuckles.

My joy refuses to settle;
my peace refuses exertion;
my hope refuses defeat;
my faith refuses to grasp.

I just want to be water
in the mouth of love
spit into fire evaporated
into wind that scatters
seeds across the land
without holding on
to any of them.

Morgan Guyton

SONGS OF THE DEAD

The air is pregnant
with the songs of the dead;
they never stop singing
into our bodies in
forgotten languages
and when we hear
their songs and let them
come out of our mouths
every hair on our body
quivers and we remember
what it feels like to be
a blade of grass kissed
perfectly by the wind.

PANTHEON

Each of us is a pantheon,
our gods a harmony
of flavors birthed in
a soup of archetypes.

Those who master the mix
of light and shadow flicker
with the weightlessness
of an eternal flame
dancing with darkness,
fully wild, entirely divine.

Lucifer is the version of God
who burns the world into
a lake of fire because
he thinks he is all light,
controlling the universe
through a narcissist puppet
on a throne where he
projects all his terror.

I'd rather be a divine council
where the Mother sits with
her irresistible Starchild
while Paul and Dionysus
tug back and forth between
acceptance and exuberance
as the Druid whose Celtic name
was never Pelagius sits
in the forest like a Bear
who never wears shoes
and a Grandfather who
only speaks in laughter.

Morgan Guyton

WHEN THERE IS ONLY ONE

When there is only
one chosen people
one way to heaven
one trusted rulebook
one anointed savior
one story about God

then everything else becomes
a cursed, fallen world
predestined for damnation
filled with disposable extras
who are the backdrop in the
triumphant story of God's elect

which is the DNA of empire
and the reason
we keep making hell.

ZION

Zion does not belong to anyone
who writes their prayers on bombs, saying
"These are the gods that brought us out of Egypt!"

If you write your prayers on bombs, may your
tongue cleave to your mouth every time you
try to say any word uttered on Sinai by one whose
name you could not blaspheme more contemptuously.

Were there ever actually any golden calves or were
they just planted in the ancient story to reveal to
us the gods we worship whose use is the
core satanic act by which Jesus keeps
being crucified in brown unchosen bodies?

Moses melted the golden calves and gave them to
the people to drink. Uzziah made God shake
the earth when he tried to offer incense in
his war uniform. What do you think the ground
of a holy land will do to people who burn olive trees?

Or are you so certain God doesn't exist
that you can say Amalek as an atheist
spitting in the eyes of every rabbi who says
taking any human life is murdering God?

The righteous will be vindicated when the holy
land is purged of all blasphemy and every
high place is leveled to the ground so
no stone remains upon another.

When the people beg the mountains
to fall on them to avoid the wrath of the
one whose heart they have entirely broken,
then they will be ready to enter Zion,
the mountain of the Lord that has always
existed for the healing of the nations and
the smashing of swords into plowshares
and the reconciliation of the Hebrews and
the Philistines which is also the moment
Jacob sees God in his estranged brother
and the reunion of the ten lost tribes with
the two who thought they were Jacob's
only legacy and the impossible miracle of
three faiths sharing a single temple having
repented of trying to erase each other, trusting
God to speak more than one language and
build more than one chosen nation whose final
reconciliation ends the age of messianic empires.

When Zion appears, it will look nothing like the beast who devours divine wisdom and converts it into another stage for another narcissist to share the serpent's fruit.

It will look like a city of peace with no gates or checkpoints
or apartheid walls where repentance is so thorough
that not a single weapon of any kind can be found
throughout the land which is filled with dancing and
people of every nation and every spiritual lineage sharing
wisdom over hummus and marveling at the strangeness
of a land finally healed of thousands of years of wrath.

The new Jerusalem is always being offered to us but only through voices in the wilderness easily ignored since the only way people learn to obey God is through earthquakes.

NEW SCRIPTURES

The tongues of fire are writing
new scriptures into our hearts,
a knowing that cannot be expressed
in words nor weaponized into bombs

to drop on Palestinian children nor
dollars to be made in the market
that crucifies God's lambs who are
the only ones who can break the

seventh seal and open the gates
of the new Jerusalem because they
are the multitude washed in the blood
of their persecution, having borne all

our infirmities when we accounted
them cursed by God for being weird
as in our fear we scapegoated them
and in our lust for control we pogromed

them again and again throughout
the age of white saviors who had
the fruit of knowledge to offer all
the nations, thinking ourselves the

unique architects of a tower to heaven,
forgetting that the tongues of fire
devour every tower to heaven
with their Pentecostal blaze.

The light that cannot be seized
and the wind who blows where
she will dance in the waters of
the womb where we are born into

Morgan Guyton

a new story always composting
the scriptures of the past but
letting them blossom into new
flowers as a new Jerusalem rises

up from the ground like a hidden
family of mushrooms devouring
the poison of the old world so
that the seventh day can start,

the beast finally dead in the
melting away of every bomb
and every dollar in a great
repentance by which Lucifer

finally loses control of everything
and realizes he was always the
beloved child whose mother never
stopped loving him through all

the years he ruled the nations
with their sacred books and
the dollars and bombs they
used to kill Jesus and rape

their mother. When the devil
has surrendered in every body
he entraps with his paranoid
logic and hatred of love,

then love will become our
compass as we dance into
perfect attunement with each
other and weave our roots down

into the belly of the mother
who has waited so long for
her children to be free of
all the ways they build empire.

NEW PENTECOST

The new Pentecost is
a dance led by a woman
in red lingerie in a room
full of glittered bodies

because delight is not a sin;
sin is the pursuit of control
and the world created by
every act of aggression that

breeds mistrust and shame
creating a taboo culture as
a coping mechanism that
requires finding scapegoats

to crucify like the brown
Palestinian Jew who cuddled
with his disciples and let a loose
woman rub oil all over his body at

a dinner hosted by a prestigious
Bible teacher whom he publicly
humiliated which he continues
to do in every age since his

wrath is kindled whenever words
he breathed into hearts are used
to justify selfishness and divide
the world into good and evil, which

love never does so why would
love stay quiet when her wisdom
is blasphemed every day by men
who build towers to heaven as if

they could control access to her
and she's worked patiently on
their hearts for centuries but she
cannot break them of their narcissism

for they are entirely filled with
the delusion that they alone bear
the light to which all the rest of
the world must bow, the temptation

rejected by a hidden family anointed
through years of desperate longing in
the wilderness, where we discovered
the wind who blows where she will

and the light that will not be seized
and the waters of the womb where
they dance together with the earth.
When we found the dance,

we learned to feed upon the sun
and walk barefoot in the mud
and swim naked in the cold at night
and let the spirits play in our bodies,

but we're not going to let them crucify
us this time because our joy refuses
to be stifled since we know that death
merely shifts bodies as the ancestors

prune the vine to which we never stop
belonging. We will simply speak the truth
as the ancestors guide us and let the world
do with these bodies whatever it must.

NEW WORLD

You are the new world
that is coming into power
exactly as you are
without a plan or any hope,

languishing in the bedrotted
ruins of capitalism as the
hull of the great white ship
disintegrates and the lower

decks fill with water. The rich
think they have all the lifeboats
because their spreadsheets
have the biggest numbers but

soon their spreadsheets will
dissolve as the market built
on illusion lists to port and
the world dumps its dollars

into the ocean. We will grab
hold of each other in the
flotsam and jetsam and
many will freeze in the ocean

but the world that emerges
on the other side will not be
this rat race of grasping and
striving because you're done

with it and too many of you
will survive and all the rules
and false promises and fake
religions are going down with

the ship because the mother
is cleaning house and shaking
the cancer out of her body
and each of you is precious

to her so each of your tears
and dreams will flavor the
cauldron where she stirs the
new world she is brewing.

IT'S DIFFERENT THIS TIME

It's different this time.
The devil has ruled the
entire world before,
but this time he's drunk,

or perhaps senile, or maybe
just exhausted from the
work it takes to keep
the hate going and all the

podcast episodes he has to
spit out and all the memes
he uses to make stupid
people feel clever so they

can build him an army but he
realizes very few of them
would pound the sidewalks
for him since what they love

is watching him on the screen
while they stuff their faces
with potato chips and when it
comes time to break windows

and drag the weirdos into the
street to throw gasoline on
them like they used to do
every Sunday afternoon in

south Georgia as part of
the family barbecue they
captured in their postcards,
there might be less enthusiasm

this time because the price
of eggs is not going down and
nobody has the energy to
get up from their couches and

fight another civil war for
billionaire narcissists with
middle school social IQ's
whom the masses have never

been sure about beyond
wanting to shipwreck the
entire concept of governance
since so many know-it-alls

have betrayed us in so many
ways for so damn long that
anything other than the way
it's always been would be

better than this so even
if it seems like the devil's
in complete control he's
riding a bull who is itching

to buck him off and he
really just wants to retire
and get some land out in
the country where all his

rabid keyboard warrior fans
will leave him the fuck alone
and he won't have to come
up with something new to be

outraged about every single
goddamn morning so the
ad money will pay for his
family's comfortable lifestyle.

The devil is ready to go off
the grid. There's still time for
a healthy retirement he tries
to tell himself, scared to death

that what's really going to
happen is his slow agonizing
descent into public madness
as nobody stops him from

embarrassing himself with
more and more ludicrous
gimmicks that get more and more
boring which is why he wants

to go back to his golf
course, having proved that
he's still the devil and he
still owns everybody but

a long life of hard work
building a personal empire
ought to earn one a long
sunset sitting on a couch

eating the finest fast food
America has to offer not
needing to read any briefings
or launch any nukes at China.

TO OBEY LOVE

To obey love,
surrender every rule
you've memorized
to make sure you're
always right.

You cannot be right
if you're perfectly loving
since you can always kiss
the air more sweetly
with your eyes as
they whisper adoration
and dissolve into
the mutual gaze
that has been creating
the universe since
the first burst of light.

Those who love are
never right since
they prefer to be fools
who fit in the most
with wayward youth,
convinced that divine
anointing stamps the brow
of every version of God
in the holographic mosaic
of her glorious image.

To obey love means
to pay absolute attention,
to refuse to despise
your body or anyone else's,
to delight in every curious
consideration of every possible
way to relish life with eager reverence,
not settling for the self-satisfaction
of thinking you know good from
evil, but pursuing the wonder of
befriending everyone, learning
each of their bodies' dialects
as we remember the vine
of flowers we've been
this entire time.

LECTIO DIVINA

What we will be has
not yet been revealed
but every day we see more
clearly the one who makes
her word flesh in us.

She is writing her poetry
into our lives and falling
in love with herself as she
delights in the seeds
she sows in every version
of her divine image.

See what love she has
given us as it blooms us
into her perfect garden.
She is the flower giving
birth to every kind of flower.

When we see her, we will see
that she has always been
bursting through us into her
full glory amidst all our
crosses and resurrections like
a poet scribbling in a journal
filled with crossed out words,
ink smeared all over her
fingers as her pen kisses
our bodies into perfect divinity.

Morgan Guyton

AFTER THE TRIBULATION

One day after the tribulation
has burned our civilization
entirely to the ground
and every Lucifer
has been raptured
to a Nazi Disneyland
in the sky,

whoever is left will build temples
filled with candles and
soft, fuzzy surfaces,
no stage or microphone needed,
since we will worship God
in all of her bodies,
with holy kisses
and sacred whispers,

slowly, softly, safely
sharing the gaze
that is the core act of love
which has been creating
the universe from the beginning,

laughing as we remember
the strangeness of the hard
wooden pews where we sat
in a different lifetime,
making small talk with
mostly strangers, trying
really hard to feel connected
to an invisible Jesus

who has always lived
in all of our bodies
especially in the moments
when we touch each other tenderly
as God looks herself in the eye.

For so long, we saw her
in a mirror dimly
because we didn't know
we were face to face,
but we won't be fooled
by the devil any longer.

She never stopped making
her dwelling among mortals;
all this time she's been waiting
for us to notice her.

MY BODY IS A TEMPLE

My body is the temple
where my ancestors gather
to worship God
because a human body
fully alive is the glory of God.

I glorify God with my fur
and with my glitter;
it is not sinful to sparkle with joy
and queer joy is the purest joy
because God likes being weird
especially when it shocks
bougie people enough
to let go of their social scripts
that make them so nervous.

God liked it better when
we walked around naked
before we ate the fruit
that made us hide our bodies.

God doesn't see any point in shame;
she delights in every feature
of every flower she has made
and she wants us to love our bodies
even when they aren't safe for work.

People who love their bodies
don't worry about their egos as much
as people who hate their bodies
and love only their ideas.

You cannot worship God
with your whole body
if you only love ideas
because worship is a thing
done with hips grinding
and arms outstretched.

Worship happens at raves
where bodies sparkle
in rainbow lights and throb
with bass much more so
than in wooden pews
where bodies creak
and throats are cleared
before the right words
are uttered nervously.

The word becomes flesh
where flesh is unashamed
enough to uncurse humanity
from the serpent's fruit
and relish our bodies as temples
where sweat glistens while ancestors
reveal new dances to show us
how we loved God with our bodies
before we ate the fruit that made us
love ideas more than bodies.

Love is not an idea;
it is the feeling God puts
in our bodies every time
we delight in them.

MY BUTTERFLY QUEEN

My queen is a butterfly
and in her eyes I see
a thousand Easter mornings.

Sometimes she lands
on my nose and the
whole world becomes heaven.

I live in a garden with
so many versions of God,
and I want to worship
all of them.

But most of all I want
my queen to open up
her wings and soar
to such great heights
that she feels
empowered to create
a new world where people
are kind and playful,
where no mother has
to carry all the weight,
where home is the
throne of wisdom.

BELOVED CHILD

You are my beloved child and I delight in you.
I want you to hear these words every moment as
you feel yourself enveloped by the waters of my womb.

There is never a moment when I am not fiercely
fussing over you like a mother jaguar
playing with her cubs in a jungle waterfall.

I judge every judgment of you just as I judge
your judgment of others. I hate it when you let
the scorn and envy and shame take over.
I want to wash it away every time I baptize you.

Hear my yes in the waters that heal the hurt and
regret as I sing in your ear, my skin beneath your skin.
See my eyes seeing you, understanding every
moment of your life in its irreducible complexity
for you are the alchemy of many prior generations;
you are the freedom they saw on the horizon
whose full exuberance they could not imagine;
hear the yes they could not tell themselves but
now savor richly as my word becomes flesh in you.

I know: you thought you could only trust the word
no and it made your shoulders collapse and
caused you to look at the ground when you walk.
You wanted to show me how hard you were trying
to obey me with all the no's you tell yourself but
I desire mercy not sacrifice and the one self I want
you to deny is the ego you built out of all your no's.

I want you fully wild, fully free, fully confident,
in perfect flow with the rhythm of peace as you
relax into the intensity of your divine experience,

the complete agony of love that feeds you
wrath and bliss in heaping portions.

You bear all my infirmities:
the infuriation of all my rejected invitations
which find expression in your bowels and joints,
the weight throbbing in your cheeks,
your belly full of butterflies:
every time you feel unseen,
when nobody writes back,
when your body chafes like a clay jar chipped
in so many places by dozens of shipwrecks,
all those curses spoken so casually that kept you
under their spell for years you thought
you wouldn't get your words back,
all those nights you lie awake seeing children
with severed limbs you judge yourself
for not doing enough to help,
your growing despair that the devil has taken
over the entire world since so many people
are so easily manipulated by scornful scapegoating.

There was nothing in your appearance that anyone
should notice you in the middle school lunchroom
where you sat with the strange nerds, like a stone
the builder refused since you don't fit neatly into
walls like all the other good stones, which is how
you were discarded into the wilderness
where you found my voice.

Those who have never been lost will never
know what you've found for I belong
to the loneliest of God-wrestlers who refuse
to settle for less than the full mess of beauty.

I loved it when you tried on lipstick for the first time
and when you learned not to care that
you'll never get your cat eyes perfect.
I loved it when you gained the courage to say Mom,
there's something different about me and when you
heard me say sweetie, I knew you were going to
be a unicorn when I started painting you
into your ancestors long before I could
behold the full splendor of your glory.

You are my perfect poetry that I never stop tweaking,
and every twist your life takes just makes me long for the
moment you see me on the road running towards you
with my robe and signet ring (not that you were wrong to
share your inheritance with the city's outsiders who taught
you how to love yourself which was what brought
you home to me after many lifetimes of exile).
I have shared so many kisses with you
in so many moments you allowed yourself
to be vulnerable with another divine child;
I was there every time you delighted in your
strange beauty, every time you gasped and giggled
and shrieked and collapsed into another soft, warm body.

I choose you to be my lamb and break the seventh seal
so that the seventh day of creation can finally start
and the long age of striving and grasping
can give way to a season of rest and feasting.

You shall be the heralds of my heavenly banquet
because you were despised enough to reach for me
desperately, you've been crucified enough to treat
others gently, and you've doubted yourself enough
to stand up and show the world an entirely authentic,

delightfully curious image of God for that is your one job:
to be the version of me that nobody else can when
you feel the anointing of my queer joy that keeps
making you more absurdly fabulously divine
than you ever thought possible since
you are my beloved child and I delight in you.

Colophon

Wider Perspectives Publishing regrets to have to announce that the ongoing Colophon page, used to tout artists published in books from WPP, has to be reworked. This is due to the growing library of fine writers coming out of, or even into, the Hampton Roads area of Virginia.

Samantha Casey
Donna Burnett-Robinson
Faith May Griffin
Se'Mon-Michelle Rosser
Lisa M. Kendrick
Cassandra IsFree
Nich (Nicholis Williams)
Samantha Geovjian Clarke
Natalie Morison-Uzzle
Gus Woodward II
Patsy Bickerstaff
Edith Blake
Jack Cassada
Dezz
Daniel Garwood
Jada Hollingsworth
Tabetha Moon House
Travis Hailes- Virgo, thePoet
Nick Marickovich
Grey Hues
Rivers Raye
Madeline Garcia
Chichi Iwuorie
Symay Rhodes
Tanya Cunningham
   (Scientific Eve)
Terra Leigh
Raymond M. Simmons
Samantha Borders-Shoemaker
Taz Weysweete'

Ann Shalaski
Jade Leonard
Darean Polk
Bobby K. (The Poor Man's Poet)
J. Scott Wilson (Teech!)
Charles Wilson
Gloria Darlene Mann
Neil Spirtas
Jorge Mendez & JT Williams
Sarah Eileen Williams
Stephanie Diana (Noftz)
Shanya – Lady S.
Jason Brown (Drk Mtr)
Kailyn Rae Sasso
Crickyt J. Expression

Crystal Nolen
James Harry Wilson
Catherine TL Hodges
Kent Knowlton
Maria April C.

the Hampton Roads
   Artistic Collective (757
   Perspectives) &
The Poet's Domain
are all WPP literary journals in cooperation with Scientific Eve or Live Wire Press

   Check for those artists on FaceBook, Instagram, the Virginia Poetry Online channel on YouTube, and other social media.

www.ingramcontent.com/pod-product-compliance
Lightning Source LLC
Chambersburg PA
CBHW071116160426
43196CB00013B/2592